In The Lan
Cried Te
Grandma's Story

By Avis Turner

Thanks you
Avis Turner

LHP

ISBN-13: 978-1468071023

ISBN-10: 1468071025

Laurel Hill Publishing LLC
Thomas D. Perry
P. O. Box 11
4443 Ararat Highway
Ararat, Virginia 24053
www.freestateofpatrick.com
freestateofpatrick@yahoo.com
276-692-5300

Cover image is oil painting of family farm by Ida Ruth.

Contents

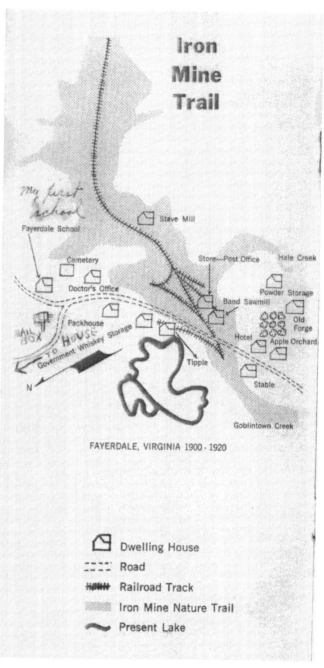

Iron Mine Trail

my first school

Fayerdale School

Stave Mill

Cemetery

Store—Post Office

Hale Creek

Doctor's Office

Powder Storage

Band Sawmill

Old Forge

Packhouse

Hotel

Apple Orchard

MAIL BOX

TO HOUSE

Government Whiskey Storage

Tipple

Stable

N

Goblintown Creek

FAYERDALE, VIRGINIA 1900-1920

Dwelling House

Road

Railroad Track

Iron Mine Nature Trail

Present Lake

Note the present location of Fairy Stone Lake covering the railroad.

1. IRON MINE

The area in the valley at the foot of this hill has been the center of activity for several years. At varying intervals for the past one hundred and fifty years there has been Iron Mining, a boom-town Fayerdale, lumbering, whiskey making, and the Civilian Conservation Corps during the development of the park.

This hill and some of the surrounding hills are honeycombed with old Iron Mines that once produced the finest iron ore obtainable. Most of the mine shafts have been covered over by land slides as has this one. However, there are a few that have remained open, and you will see one further along the trail.

On this trail you will see evidence of this early civilization. Consult the accompanying map reconstructing the town of Fayerdale.

Courtesy of Fairy Stone State Park

Closed up mine for iron ore at Fairy Stone State Park.

Prologue

I remember my grandmother's golden earrings and listening to her telling about the gypsy's prediction of her marrying my grandfather the sixth time she saw him.

Grandma Hollandsworth lived with my family for as long as I can remember. She was the only grandparent I knew---the other three died young, but I do remember one great grandfather Joshua Thomas Carter who lived to be 94 (1852-1946) and visited his grandchildren every so often.

I began my genealogy hobby in 1960, Grandma died in 1958. There are so many things I wish I had asked her when I had the chance. Grandma's story began by asking questions of my mother, Ida Ruth, who was the youngest child, only two when her father died. I interviewed all of Grandma's six living children and three of her brothers. My mother and Minnie Lou drew pictures of the old farm home and illustrated some of the stories. I have an oil painting my mother did of the rented farmhouse and surrounding land.

Most of Grandma's story is how she and her family survived after the death of her husband. It was 1915 and they were living in the Fayerdale area known for gunfights, making moonshine, iron mines, lumber, and railroad work.

When the mine shut down, Mr. J. B. Fishburn of Roanoke (an associate of lumber company president Frank A. Hill), bought all the stock, and became sole proprietor. Later, Mr. Fishburn gave the land to the state for a park. The park's name Fairy Stone came from the legend of the crosses found in the area.

My mother and I collected the natural fairystones and sold them at craft shows we participated in, or gave them free with purchase. "Staurolites" is the geological term for fairystones. They can be filed, shaped, and made into necklaces and keychains. Sometimes they are polished with linseed oil for a dark color. A jeweler can add gold tips and chain to make a lovely necklace. I enjoy the compliments received when I wear mine. The following is the legend that I typed to go with the beautiful fairystones.

Legend of the Fairy Stones

Hundreds of years before King Powhatan's dynasty came into power, long before the woods breathed the gentle spirit of the lovely Pocahontas, the fairies were dancing around a spring of limpid water playing with naiads and wood nymphs when an elfin messenger arrived from a strange city, far, far away, bringing the sad tidings of the death of Christ.

When these creatures of the forest heard the terrible story of the crucifixion, they wept. As the tears fell upon the earth, they were crystallized into little pebbles on each of which was formed a beautiful cross. When the fairies disappeared from the enchanted spot, the ground about the spring and the adjacent valley was strewn with these unique mementoes of that melancholy event.

For many years, thousands of people have held these little crosses of stone in a more or less superstitious awe, being firm in the belief that they will protect the wearer against witchcraft, sickness, accidents, and disasters of all kinds. All the stones have the shape of a cross. Many of them are of the St. Andrew's variety, others are Roman, and some are the Maltese.

Fayerdale is now called Fairy Stone State Park. The park was developed by the Civilian Conservation Corps (CCC) by order of President Franklin D. Roosevelt—one of his favorite New Deal projects. In 1933, the CCC built the dam on Goblintown Creek to create Fairy Stone Lake. Fairy Stone is one of six original parks built and one of the most popular. We had a club picnic (Fieldale High School) at Fairy Stone Park in 1952. Nowadays, all the printed information, highway signs, etc. have Fairy Stone (two words) Park. The boomtown of Fayerdale is now covered with water.

Elmer Haynes said it best in *The Fayerdale Tragedy Fairy Stone State* Park © 1983. "Today, the sounds of train whistles, pick axes, and drunken brawls are virtually gone from these hills. They have been replaced by sounds of children swimming in the lake, crackling campfires, and curious hikers."

--Avis Turner, Bassett, Virginia, 2011

Ida Ruth at the cabin where she was born.

Descending Family Tree

Shadrack Turner married Ann _____
Born 1720   Born ca 1723
(9 children) 4th child was

William Turner* married Jane Hunter
Born 1-12-1753   Born 1763
(14 children) 12th child was

Josiah Turner, Sr. married Drucilla Philpott
Born 12-09-1784   Born 8-1794
(12 children) 4th child was

Josiah Turner, Jr. married Malinda Ruth Ingram
Born 3-11-1822   Born 11-13-1831
(13 children) 3rd child was

Robert Turner married Sarah Ellen Martin
(18 children-including 4 from 2nd marriage)
4th child was Martha Ellen Turner

*Names of militiamen who marched to the assistance of Col. Green at
Guilford Court House, March 11, 1781

Abram Penn, Col. Commanding

John Cunningham's Company

Joseph Cunningham   Nathan Beal
Munford Perryman   *William Turner
*Thomas Hollandsworth   Samuel Packwood
Reuben Webster   Daniel Smith
Josiah Turner (William's brother, b. 1753, son
of Shadrack)

Thomas Hollandsworth, Sr.* married Susannah Born 1740-1750
Maze (Mays)
(5 children) 3rd child was

11

Thomas Hollandsworth, Jr. married Patsy
Born 1770-1780   Craddock
                          Born 1780-1790
(2 children I know of) 1st child was

William Hollandsworth married Frances Spencer
Born 2-12-1807   Born 7-10-1810
(7 children) 4th child was

John Jackson Hollandsworth** married Orpah
Born 4-21-1838   Anne Cahill
                          Born 1-13-1845
(11 children) 7th child was
Thomas Alexander Hollandsworth

**Jack Hollandsworth enlisted in the Confederate Army at age 25 on August 1, 1863 at Christiansburg, Virginia in Montgomery County. He was a Private in Company K, 22nd Regiment, Virginia Cavalry, McAustin's Brigade. Enlistment was for a period of three years. His Captain was John Francis. After serving for a little over one year, he was captured at Strasburg, September 23, 1864. J. J. Hollandsworth's name appeared on a Roll of Prisoners of War at Harper's Ferry, West Virginia, captured by General Sheridan's Forces, and sent to Point Lookout, Maryland on September 30, 1864. He arrived at Harper's Ferry October 3, 1864. He died February 13, 1920, age 82.

Turner Genealogy

A little girl was born February 27, 1880, in Franklin County, Virginia just over the Patrick County line, in a house up in the hollow behind the old France home place. Martha Ellen Turner was the fourth child of 14 children born to Robert called "Robin" Turner, a farmer and blacksmith, and Sarah Ellen (Martin) Turner. She was a midwife and helped deliver many babies in the Dodson community. She joined Union Church in 1887; she wrote poetic obituaries that were published in religious magazines.

Sarah Ellen died May 23, 1907, age 52. Robin remarried to Suzie Craddock, she was about 20, and he was in his 50s. They had four children. Robin Turner died in 1915, age 63. Suzie married again to a Mize, again to a Draper, and again to a Cockram.

Hollandsworth Genealogy

A little boy was born in nearby Franklin County, Virginia—Brown Hill section near Ferrum. Twins—a boy and a girl—born to John Jackson Hollandsworth and Orpah Anne (Cahill) Hollandsworth, sixth and seventh of 11 children, on July 26, 1876—11 years after the end of the "Civil" War.

Virginia Evelyn, called "Jenny" and Thomas Alexander, called "Tom" were their names. Their father was a war veteran. This was near the end of the Reconstruction Period (1865-1877). "J. J." as he was called (and sometimes "General Jackson" nickname), survived Gettysburg battles, and Point Lookout, Maryland, prison. Then, he married in 1866, raised his family, farmed the land, and went to Union

13

Primitive Baptist Church in Patrick County. It was there Tom
Hollandsworth met a pretty, young woman named Martha, called
"Mattie," Turner. He would soon learn of the gypsy's prediction.

Mattie Hollandsworth

The Gypsy

Once upon a time, there was a young woman named Martha Ellen Turner, called "Mattie." She lived with her father Robert called "Robin" Turner and mother, Sarah Ellen (Martin) Turner in Franklin County, Virginia along with her nine brothers and sisters (two boys died young, two children not yet born).

Mattie—everyone called her that—worked hard, as they all did on the farm near the foot of the Blue Ridge Mountains. She was only 18 in the spring of 1898 and already an accomplished cook, and made especially good biscuits and gravy!

When the gypsy wagon came rolling down the country road, Mattie decided to have her ears pierced. She chose the small, golden earrings that glittered in the sun.

The encyclopedia tells us a gypsy's ancestors probably came from India many years ago, later reached Europe, and crossed over to North America. Most gypsy families continued their nomadic existence, however some settled down. They were known for music and dancing; their bright embroidered clothing; gold jewelry and bangles; bold pranks and taking things. Not all gypsies led this kind of life, not all gypsies were dishonest it said. I believe some gypsy families had settled in the counties of Franklin and Patrick.

The next spring—1899—Mattie had her fortune told when the gypsy lady made her return trip. I can picture it now. Mattie, listening attentively as the gypsy held her hand to read her palm. The gypsy told her that soon she would meet her future husband. "He will be in a crowd," she said. Then she said he was not too tall, had dark hair—

15

described exactly how he would look. The gypsy went on to say, "The second time you see him, he will be with another girl. The third time he will go home with you. And the sixth time you see him, you will be married!" Mattie didn't believe a word of it. She thought she would probably marry the young man she was going with then. But—the next month at church, she met a man—he was not too tall, and had dark hair; he matched the gypsy's description perfectly! His name was Thomas Alexander Hollandsworth.

A month or so later, the second time Mattie saw Thomas Alexander Hollandsworth, he was with another girl. Moreover, the third time she saw Tom Hollandsworth, he went home with the Turner family for dinner after the Sunday meeting at Union Church in nearby Patrick County. They were married January 18, 1900—the sixth time she ever saw him!

Many years later Mattie Turner Hollandsworth, now shortened to Mat (Sister Mat, Aunt Mat), enjoyed recalling her teen years, and showing the golden earrings she never took out. She told grandchildren about the gypsy and the fortune—how she met her husband and the gypsy's prediction came true. They called it a "whirlwind courtship" and she would remind them it was a month or two between their meetings. Then, with a twinkle in her eye, Mattie said Tom kissed her for the <u>first</u> time after one week of marriage!

Tom, Mattie, and Family

Tom Hollandsworth was a fine-looking man. He had black, wavy hair, and a mustache. He and his twin sister were born July 26, 1876. Tom was 23 years old when he married Mattie, who was almost 20. She wore her dark hair pulled back, showing a widow's peak (said to foretell early widowhood). Tom and Mattie welcomed their first child, a daughter, born nine months and 16 days after their marriage. They named her Orpah (after Tom's mother, Orpah Cahill) Virginia Evelyn (after Tom's twin sister) and called her "Jennie."

Jennie had pretty, blonde hair, long—way below her shoulders. She was small, but acted very "growny," so particular. The little family was happy. About three years later, a son was born—James Robert—August 12, 1903. Then, about six months later Jennie died of scarlet fever. A sad day for all, including the extended family of grandparents, aunts, uncles, friends, and neighbors.

This obituary was printed in "The Messenger of Truth," written by Mattie's mother October 1904.

Miss Jennie Hollandsworth

My granddaughter, and daughter of T. A. and Mattie E. Hollandsworth, was born November 13, 1900, and died February 5, 1904 of Scarlet Fever. She was the most obedient child I ever saw of her age. Her ways were more like a grown lady than a child. She was very small for her age. Some said she looked so much like a doll they did not think she would ever be raised.

My darling little granddaughter who was so near to me;
 And now her little antic ways I never more can see;
But can see her little playthings and all her little toys,
 And ought not to wish her back away from all her joys.

That dear little form; how still it doth lie,
 For its happy little spirit went shouting away,
Away to the Savior in heaven above,
 Away from suffering to dwell in love.

O, how we do miss the sweet little girl,
 But she is gone from this troublesome world.
No more to suffer nor shed a tear
 For she is gone to glory where there is no fear.

And while we were around her grave,
 We ask the Lord our souls to save
That we may meet once more again,
 There forever more to remain.

While its poor mother doth mourn and weep,
 It is praising the Savior, O, how sweet.
If she could hear its sweet little voice,
 She then would surely have to rejoice.

Dodson, Virginia   Mrs. Sarah E. Turner

   Tom and Mattie had five more children: John Peter, born May
11, 1905; Minnie Lou, born August 17, 1907; Thomas Green, born July 7
1909; Mattie Lee, born February 14, 1911; and Ida May, born January
20, 1913. They were busy—farming and raising the children. There
were few cross words between them. He was strict with the children.
They said he never scolded them—didn't have to. One look from their
father and they knew they better behave. John said they moved from

Franklin County to Patrick County, on Shooting Creek, and lived there about two years, then moved to Fayerdale.

Living in a Boom-Town

Tom was a farmer, but he also worked for several years at the sawmill in Fayerdale. They lived in a four-room frame house. They rented the company house from the Virginia Ore and Lumber Co. (John said it changed hands several times, and probably names, too). Frank A. Hill was president of the lumber company. Mr. Hill's wife gave the town its name—using "F" of her husband's name and "Ayer" his middle name, and then "Dale" being the middle name of an associate, H. Dale Lafferty of New York City.

The town grew up amid iron mining, lumbering, and whisky-making activities—its population was about 2,000 in 1900: "400 mine workers and over 1,000 lumber and railroad employees," said Elmer Haynes in his book on *The Fayerdale Tragedy*. The town was also known for gunfights and several murders stemming from drunken brawls, reporting on illegal stills, jealousy, etc.—sounds like an Old West Movie. Elmer Haynes told of the shooting death of Euel Cox, prosperous farmer, merchant, and bootlegger; surviving were his wife Mae Turner Cox, and his only child, Minnie Cox. He was ambushed September 5 and died September 6, 1922. There were other shootings through the years—three dead, two wounded in 1927.

There were iron mines—the Hairston family produced pig iron in and around Stuart's Knob. Tom Elgin ran the post office and store. This was a combination general store, post office, and railroad depot, according to Fairy Stone State Park Brochure, The Iron Mine Trail. "Most transactions were through barter, trading products of the land, tanbark, crossties, chestnuts, walnuts, and such for merchandise." Tom Burnette was the conductor on the train in Fayerdale.

There was a hotel. Also, a doctor's office, livery stable, boarding house (this is where Dr. Albert C. Lancaster lived—his office was near the school and pack house), several houses, and a school (it used to be an old forge—iron ore was stored there and served as a dwelling house as well).

Dr. Lancaster got the first car in Fayerdale—a Ford "Model T." When they heard him coming, everyone would run to the road and watch him go by—they had never seen a car before.

The Hollandsworth family attended primitive Baptist churches—Old Union, Knob and others that met once a month. When Mattie joined the church at Knob, Tom said he was not going to the baptizing. Mattie was to be baptized in the river at Old Union because there was nowhere for a baptizing at Knob. He went off to pitch horseshoes with friends. Tom changed his mind, and got to the river as the preacher and Mattie were in the water, just before baptizing her. Tom walked in the water, joined the church, and they were baptized together. Some people thought he went in because he was afraid Mattie would drown—they didn't know he had asked for a home with the church and wanted to be baptized, too.

The Missing Year

No one talked about 1915—except, that is the year Tom Hollandsworth died—December 2, 1915. One of his children said his father "went to West Virginia to work for awhile." One cousin was told the story after she was grown and married. Another overheard the conversation with a preacher in the next room. Tom Hollandsworth died while in prison for a crime he did not commit, a little before his one-year sentence was up.

There was a legal distillery and many illegal whisky-making stills in the area. Elmer Haynes states in The Fayerdale Tragedy, Fairy Stone State Park: "Mining towns were notorious for their drunken brawls, and Fayerdale was no exception. Almost every family in or around Fayerdale was engaged in farming and liquor making." One of the "biggest crimes" was reporting a still to the authorities.

It must have been a hot summer day in 1914 when Tom and one of his sons were both working in their cornfield. They wore large farm hats to protect them from the sun's rays. All of a sudden, a man came running into the field, and threw his hat down; he kept running. Lawmen are next; they stop and pick up the hat, and ask Tom, "Is this your hat?"

He replied, "No, I've got my hat on." When asked, he said, "That is not my still."

The still was on land that adjoined the farm that Tom rented, and he was arrested. At the trial, the judge asked Tom, "Is that your still?"

He replied, "No sir, it is not. I admit that I had a still once, a lo time ago, but that is not my still." He would not tell whose still it was. He knew, but feared for his life and for his family's safety. The judge sentenced Tom to serve one year in prison.

That may be when the family moved to the old log farmhouse. The warden sent a nice condolence letter to Mattie saying that her husband had a heart attack. He put his hands over his chest and cried out, "Oh, my heart, I'm dying." The death certificate states a physician attended the deceased, Thomas Hollingsworth (sic), from November 20 1915, to December 2, 1915, and that death occurred at 6 p.m. on Dec. 2. The body was brought from Moundsville, West Virginia by Wells Fargo Company Express on December 3 to Henry, Virginia in care of Mrs. Mattie Hollingsworth (sic).

Tom Hollandsworth

A Piece of Bread

Tom and Mattie Hollandsworth were happily married for almost 16 years. Suddenly the father, the husband, the breadwinner was gone. Mattie Hollandsworth became a widow on December 2, 1915 when Tom died of a heart attack at the young age of 39. His twin sister died the year before on July 29, 1914, age 38. Both Tom and Virginia Evelyn, who married a Haymaker, are buried in the Cahill Cemetery near Salt House Branch, Philpott Dam area. Robert Turner, Mattie's father, also died in 1915, age 63.

Mattie Hollandsworth was left with six children, ages ranging from two to twelve. After her husband's death, neighbors advised Mattie to give up her children—to put them in foster homes. They did not see how she was going to get along with six children to raise alone. Dr. Albert Lancaster, the company doctor, wanted four year-old Mattie Lee. Posey Jamerson wanted to take Green, age 6. He said, "You know you can't keep them all together."

Mattie thought, "As long as I have fingernails to claw and raise a garden, I'll not break up my family." Aloud, to the neighbors, she said, "As long as I have a piece of bread to divide, I'll keep my family together."

The family moved from the frame company house to a nearby farm. The log house had one big main room downstairs, and the kitchen offset was reached by going on the front porch and then into the kitchen. The kitchen had a back door also, as did the main room. There was a big room upstairs with four beds—two wooden and two iron. There was an old homemade floor chest (armoire). The boys, along with uncles Ed and Albert Turner slept upstairs. Mattie's two younger, unmarried brothers stayed with them often to help run the farm. Ed was a Private in the Army, and served nine months in World War I. It began June 28, 1914 and ended four years later on November 11, 1918—the same year as the terrible flu epidemic. Albert worked at the sawmill in Fayerdale. He said the old mine tipple and train were still there from when the company mined ore.

There were two old-fashioned wooden beds downstairs for Mattie and her three daughters. A "center table" was in the middle of the main room downstairs. The table held the oil lamp and the old family Bible from which Mattie read to her children gathered around her every night. Mattie Lee could read the New Testament before she ever went to school. Somehow, Mattie had lace curtains at one of the windows, and one crocheted doily made by Laura Ingram.

Mattie had a sewing machine. It was placed in front of the window for light to sew by in the daytime. At night, their light was mostly from the open fireplace as they could not afford much oil for the lamps. The kitchen had a small, black, wood-burning cook stove; also a flour barrel, a meal barrel, a high dish cupboard and a long homemade table with long benches and a kerosene lamp. They were afraid to heat the stove hot enough to brown the bread as there was no flue and only a pipe that went out a small window.

There was an old shed out back where Mattie's brothers built furniture. Ed and Albert made them a chest of drawers, a cupboard or two—a small one for their hats—and the wooden beds and tables. The shed was out past the chestnut tree. Two other brothers built furniture

24

too. Tom Turner made different pieces of furniture and Flem Turner made chairs.

The Hollandsworth family had no radio, no washing machine, and no electricity. There was no indoor plumbing, no outdoor plumbing, either. The rock chimney was daubed with clay. You could look out at the moon where the clay had fallen out.

Outside there was a plank walk from the porch steps across the yard. What little grass they had, was cut (mowed) with a butcher knife.

They had one mule named Jim, one cow, a hog, some chickens, and several dogs. Later they got a horse and a mule named Kate. People would try to steal chickens from them; Mattie would scare them off.

They often heard wildcats squalling around the farm at night.

Log House on the farm.
(All drawings by Ida Ruth unless otherwise noted.)

Tom, Mattie, Jim, and John Hollandsworth

Sharecropping/Earning a Living

The farm that the Hollandsworth family rented was called the "Old Hairston Land." They gave one-third of the grain, such as corn and wheat, for rent. John I. Woods was the overseer. They raised tobacco, rye, and wheat, on about 30 acres, much of that in tobacco. John said there were 20 acres in corn—they planted pole beans to run up the corn—dried the beans.

Mattie and her children earned a living in a number of ways--you could say they were "diversified." Living on a farm, they grew or raised most of their food. Some of the farm products were sold which brought them some cash for the things they had to buy. The three boys worked in the fields along with their mother and uncles.

Often the three girls were left near the fields to graze the cow while the others were working. They would pull daisies and place them in rows, and then build a pulpit and preach to those daisies. They would pretend to shake hands with the flowers. Sometimes they pulled morning glories. Minnie said they acted like they were the most well-dressed women.

On the way home from working in the garden, they carried all the weeds they could hold in their arms to feed the cow and pig. Then, they would have to get the water, which was carried by bucket from a big spring up a steep hill to the house.

They also picked blackberries, wild strawberries, and huckleberries. On the way back home, the boys Jim, John, and Green would go swimming in Goblintown Creek where Fairy Stone Lake is today. They did this to wash the chiggers off. Sometimes, Mattie would go with a group of people in the summertime to Bull Mountain to pick huckleberries to dry and sell. Sometimes the girls were chased up a tree by the cow when they were picking berries.

Mattie took in sewing. She cuffed men's pants, cleaned, and pressed suits. She patched and mended; did alterations. She was so good, when she altered a jacket, one man didn't believe she had touched it until he tried it on and found a perfect fit. The night before they moved to Bassett, she made a dress by lamplight. Once when they were "down and out"—had no money—Mattie prayed, "Send somebody with sewing." Two or three days later two women came up the road with some sewing for her to do.

The boys would search the hills for ginseng, which sold for about $13 a pound. The name, ginseng, comes from Chinese words meaning "likeness to man", because many roots are shaped like the human body. They pronounced it "gin-sang" or just "sang." Ginseng was sold to the general store and shipped to distant cities to be made into medicines. The Chinese especially, used this herb for strength, vitality, virility, rejuvenation, and longevity.

The first time they went hunting for ginseng, Mattie showed them the plant with its pretty red berries. Jim wandered off from the others, and not remembering the leaves, gathered up a supply of other plants that had red berries. He went back to his mother to show her his ginseng, and she laughed, saying, "That is not ginseng, that is Indian turnips!" John said golden root sold for $4 a pound.

The boys also picked up a little money trapping minks, muskrats, and skunks. They set rabbit traps—one morning they caught six rabbits. They hunted squirrel by day, and 'possum and 'coon at night.

Mattie's brother Sam and his two oldest children helped— plowing the garden, and he gave some money to help.

The Berry Pickers

Sisters Ruth and Mattie

"Leather Britches," etc.

Beans, beans, and more beans. They had pole beans and some called "cut shorts"—called this because they had so many short, fat beans in a pod. They had "cornfield beans," October beans, and some that resembled pinto beans, only darker. They put a quilt in the corncrib to keep the beans from going through the cracks. When the beans were dry, they would beat them out of the shells.

They picked beans by the sackful. Green beans were sold for 50 cents a bushel. Beat-out beans sold for three dollars per sack. This would buy one pair of shoes. Many years they would beat out 9 bushels of beans to eat and sell. One season they beat out 11 bushels of shelled beans. The big, main room was full of beans. There were piles of beans everywhere—about "coffee-table" high with little paths around them.

They also sold dried green beans. First, they got the strings off tender green beans. Then, they pushed a threaded needle through the center of the beans, making a long string to hang up to dry. John said Foxfire Books called these "leather britches." He said they were better than fresh beans.

Once, Mattie gave the children a lot of beans to plant and told them they could quit when all the beans were planted. The more they planted the more beans there seemed to be. There was nowhere left to plant them. So, they went out in the woods and "buried" the leftover seeds around a tree stump and under some rocks thinking that would solve the problem. In about ten days, the beans were sprouted and came up all round that tree stump. Mattie gave the children a good scolding.

Another time, Mattie and Minnie Lou started out to plant beans. She had them in her apron. Suddenly a black racer snake ran out, wrapped around Mattie's legs, and threw her down. Beans flew in every direction. Mattie kicked her feet so much it scared off the snake.

In the fall, the children could not start to school until they picked all the beans. For that is the way they bought their shoes: selling green beans, dried beans, dried berries, golden root, star root, and ginseng.

IDA RUTH CHASSED BY COW IN SNOW

a dishpan — and snow + a cow chasing you in the cow pasture
about 1928

Ida Ruth in the Dishpan Sled.

Grapevine swings, Moss Rugs and Mud Furniture

The Hollandsworth children didn't have very many toys---not bought ones anyway, but they had a lot of fun.

They had a grapevine swing near the pigpen. Jump ropes were also made from grapevines. Toy cars and wagons were made from empty spools from sewing thread. They made all kinds of little roads in the dirt for them.

They put up forked sticks with a long stick laid across and then they would jump over it. They made a see saw. For play horses they would get a pole about six feet long, tie a rope to one end for a bridle and away they went, galloping along. They would make the "horses" walk, pace, trot and run. In the summer, they went to the cool forest and bent over small trees for horses. They really had a good time riding up and down.

The girls would make up a batch of mud and shape it into little furniture. Down at the spring they would sit under the bushes, cut squares out of the ground, and make play houses. There would be several rooms. The furniture would be mud chairs, tables, and couches. In addition, there were mud pies, cakes, and beans in a mud dish with cakes of mud bread. They were dared to get mud on their dresses. Sometimes they would take rocks or boards and make larger playhouses. They covered them with moss; there were moss bedspreads, and moss rugs on the floor.

Sometimes on Sunday, the neighboring children would gather and play baseball. The ball would be made of twine and something heavy in the middle. Mattie made pancakes for all the children for a snack. Minnie Lou said, "What a feast that was."

The children enjoyed throwing rocks in the old Indian caves and iron ore mines. They had a little dog named Waddley and carried him everywhere—even to school. They dressed him up in clothes for their baby. The girls often made play houses and pretended to be their two aunts that had a new baby about every two years. Minnie Lou, Mattie Lee, and Ida Ruth made rag dolls every time one of the aunts had a new baby. They liked to dress up in old clothes, pad themselves, and laugh big to see their tummy's shake. One day they decided to play-like they were old women dipping snuff. One sneaked into the kitchen and got some cinnamon for their snuff. Boy, did they get sick of cinnamon, related Minnie Lou.

They did have a few games—they played dominoes, checkers and Rook—and Jack Rocks. If they didn't have store-bought ones, they used gravels.

Sometimes they would just sit outdoors in the chimney corners peep around the chimney at each other, and giggle. Once Minnie Lou had a songbook and wanted Mattie Lee to sing with her. She didn't want to and Minnie slapped her face and said, "Sing now!"

Once Mattie left Minnie Lou to care for the two smaller girls: Mattie Lee and Ida Ruth. For fun, she took a sack of green beans, hung them over the door, and told them it was a booger. It was nearly dark and they couldn't see, they got scared so much, Minnie Lou got scared, too. Then, they all went outdoors, down the path, and sat in the dark to wait for their mother.

34

In winter for pastime, they sat around the big open fireplace and parched corn in grease with some pepper and salt. For games, Jim made goose and gander boards (similar to Hi Q)—the goose and gander were corn and beans. As all children will do, they would cheat and fuss with each other. That is when Mattie made them put the games up for awhile.

When it snowed deep, the children loved to go outside and just fall backwards in it. They made lots of paths in the snow. The older children would slide down a steep hill on boards. Mattie Lee and Ida Ruth got dishpans out and slid in them. Sometimes the cow chased them and they would slide under the fence "just in time."

Mattie bought the old organ at Tom Foster's sale. They really thought they were "rich as need be," then. John played the organ...said he learned from the notebook that came with the organ; also by listening to others play—"by ear." Mattie Lee and Minnie Lou could play the organ, too.

One day Jim said, "Let's cuss like Ed and Albert."

John said, "No, I don't want to."

Jim said, "I'll say the first word and then you say a word." Jim said, "God."

Then John said, "Damn."

Mattie found out when John said several curse words at something he didn't like and then Jim told on him.

Children will be children, but I'm sure they both got a good scolding. Jim grew up to be a primitive Baptist preacher.

The upstairs floor had knotholes and large cracks between the planks. The little children played tricks on the others by carrying wate upstairs and looking through knotholes to pour water on someone's head downstairs. Once, sparks from the old rock chimney caught the house on fire. Minnie Lou said, "We <u>had</u> to throw water then, and worked very hard to put the fire out."

The Spring.

Onions, Cornbread, and Other Goodies

In early spring, the children would go out and gather oak balls—a pretty, light green color—from young oak trees. The balls were sweet and they ate them. The cow provided milk to drink.

For an after-school snack, the children put butter on a piece of leftover corn bread and slipped off to the onion patch to eat their buttered bread with onions. "Delicious," was their description of this treat.

From the garden came corn, beans, onions, peas, Irish potatoes, cabbage, and yams. They bought their flour. Corn was piled up in the corncrib. Neighbors came in for a "corn shucking." Mattie would fix supper for everyone. The corn was shucked and shelled to be taken to a nearby mill in sacks and ground for meal to make cornbread.

They made strawberry cake (put berries in the dough), and blackberry cobblers from berries picked on vines nearby. "Lazy" apple pies were made using big round cakes of bread dough. Pile cooked apples on circles--several layers high. Molasses cake was made by adding molasses to the dough, cooked in thin layers. It tasted much like gingerbread. Molasses and butter were mixed together and spread on a biscuit. They called this "gray horse." They also had wild apricots, huckleberries, and dewberries.

Ashcakes were cooked in a skillet in the fireplace. It was a cast iron pan with legs and a lid—to put hot coals underneath and on top, too. This was their corn bread, called ashcakes. They used hickory logs in the fireplace.

They had no meat until fall when the hog was butchered. Som
beef was bought. They would catch fish to eat using a safety pin as a
hook.

The spring was out down the hill behind the house, about 100
yards away. Milk was kept in the spring box. It was a long, wooden bc
with a lid—about two feet wide with a cement bottom-- just below the
spring. It had a hole in each end so water could run through to keep
things cold. Milk was kept in big, old stone jars. A cloth was tied arour
the top so spring lizards could not get in it. One morning they saw a bi
black bear at the spring. John ran to the house, told Jim and they got
the shotgun, and tracked the bear through the sand. The bear's foot
was "bigger than my foot," said John. They tracked him to a rock cave
and left him there.

In the fall, the Hollandsworth children gathered chinquapins by
climbing up the bush-like tree and shaking them off. Also, they
gathered chestnuts. A walnut tree was a treasure for them to find.

When fall came, potatoes were dug and then hilled away in the
ground for winter storage. A long ditch or trench was dug. Wrap in
paper or straw, cover with about six inches of dirt. The sun would heat
the dirt and keep the vegetables from freezing. Cabbage was done the
same way with roots sticking out to find one by—and turnips, too. The
did apples the same way. If they didn't have straw, they would use
leaves.

The family brined cucumbers—put salt and water and
cucumbers in a barrel to preserve them. They added watermelon,
different things to be pickled.

38

One day John decided he wanted to kill a squirrel—he was just a little fellow—never had before. He had heard two squirrels cutting in a hickory nut tree. Mattie was cooking breakfast. John goes in and says, "Mama, believe I'll go out and kill some squirrels. Will it be all right?" She said, "Yes, you're getting big enough to do something." John went out and killed those two squirrels. He was so tickled; he went back to the house. Mattie was tickled, too. "That'll be our dinner."

A creek was not too far from the house. They would catch horny head fish, no more than 12 inches long. The boys would "catch a mess of them, anytime, for food."

Once there was a small gathering at Fayerdale on the Fourth of July. Someone was selling bananas and ice cream. Mattie bought a banana, peeled it, and passed it around for each one to take a bite. The children shared a cone of ice cream this way, too. That was a wonderful treat for them.

Swinging by the Pigpen.

39

Mattie and family.

'Readin', 'Ritin', and 'Rithmetic'—the Three R's of School

Schooling was limited in those days—only 100 days and the Hollandsworth children could not go all of that as they had to plow the land for the next planting. They had to walk to school, of course. It was about a half-mile away. School was not closed because of snow. They walked to school in eight inches of snow and loved it. They also walked home for lunch, which was mostly beans and bread—and milk when the cow wasn't dry. Sometimes they took their lunch to school in a lard pail.

The first school at Fayerdale was held in an old house. Curtains divided the room. Later a two-room weatherboard school was built. Some teachers were Mrs. Sol Via, Bertha Elgin, Pearl Turner Bryant, and Nellie Wright. Alice Turner and Della Wood were two of Ida Ruth's teachers. A big wood stove heated the classroom.

There were long benches with backs. Fastened to the backside was a long shelf. The students on the front row had only their legs to hold books and papers.

The teacher gave a penny to a student every time he/she got a head mark—which was staying "ahead of the class" three times.

A spelling match was held each Friday. When you missed a word, you sat down. The last one standing was the winner.

Green learned to count by walking on the railroad tracks and counting the crossties. The first day of school he took a third grade reader; the other children all laughed. But not long, for he could read as well as the rest. In spelling, he went to the head of the class the first day.

41

At recess the children played "blindfold" (blind man's bluff), ball, and they made playhouses.

John said the first school he went to was in Dodson—about six miles away. Then a new school was built near Fayerdale. Tom Bryant was the teacher. John finished school there in 8th grade—went through it twice—nothing else to do. A teacher at school changed him from writing with his left hand—made him write with his right hand. Young sister Ida Ruth didn't wait for the teacher—the first time she saw a rule hit the hand of a left-handed student, she started writing with her right hand.

One of Ida Ruth's playmates at school was Minnie Cox, Euel Cox's daughter, she was born in 1914, Ida Ruth in 1913. Minnie later married Ellis Dodson, eight years after Euel's death.

Our Old Living Room.
(Drawing by Minnie Lou.)

42

Holidays, Neighbors, Church, Visiting

The closest church was about three miles away at Knob Church. Services were held at a different church each Sunday of the month. This was the Primitive Baptist churches. One fourth Sunday they walked four miles to Old Union Church. (This church is now under water from Philpott Dam built in the 1950s). When they finally got a horse, the children would take turns riding a little way to rest. Later, they acquired a two-horse hack, or carriage that had two seats (front and back); it would seat six people. It was called a surrey and had a square top with fringe all around. With the two mules hooked up, they were "really riding in style." Those all-day meetings were a highlight of the week. The family would take their dinner of sweet mollassy cakes and Johnny cake. In addition, they had biscuits with fried fatback.

Sometimes Mattie's sister and her family would come to visit and stay a day or two. Nancy Susan Everline (called Nan or Nannie), was four years older than Mattie. She married Josiah, called Joe, Moran, her first cousin. They had 10 children. The Hollandsworth children all looked forward to these visits, "for mama would fix something extra to eat." Once she cooked some dried corn (which back then was good) for the company. Green was a little fellow, and he was watching the company eat. He told one of them not to eat up all the corn. "And sweet potatoes and butter was the best of food."

It was a treat to go to the general store in Fayerdale. Mattie told the children to look, but not touch. They all walked around with hands behind their backs.

The closest neighbors were a mile away. Their name was Fole and they had children about the same ages. They put up a "mailbox" about halfway between the houses. The children had great fun putting letters and things in the mailbox for each other.

At Christmas time, the children all put their caps on the long bench in the kitchen behind the table—upside down. Santa would put in a few oranges, raisins, some candy, and a small toy. Minnie said, "Before dad died, we girls always got a doll." At school, the teacher passed around a box of stick candy—everyone got one stick. They had no Christmas tree or other decorations.

At Easter, they got some eggs. The children really looked forward to that. They could have all the boiled eggs they wanted. They drew pictures on the eggs and hid them like the children do today. They liked Easter better than Christmas.

Miscellaneous Personalia

<u>Clothes</u> Their clothes were made from feed sacks, washed, and bleached out. Some sacks were made with a pretty design instead of an advertisement. Sometimes they would buy print material from the store. Petticoats were made from white feed sacks with a gathered skirt and wide, heavy lace, starched stiff.

They washed their clothes down by the spring in summer. They had a big old black pot down there, some wash tubs, and a washboard. They made their own soap (lye leached from wood ashes and grease). They hung their clothes on bushes to dry. In winter, water was carried up the hill to wash at the house. Flat irons were heated on the wood stove. Ironing was done on a padded place on the kitchen table. Note: More about washday in "Looking Backward" column-see February 19, 1975.

<u>Hairstyles, Makeup</u> The girls wore their hair pulled back with a ribbon on top. Then "bangs" over the forehead came in style; when it was cut, their hair stood straight up. It finally looked okay later when their hair grew out enough to train it lay down over their forehead. The only powder they had was bath powder. Red crayons were used for rouge.

<u>Sunshine People</u> Mattie enjoyed drawing pictures and was very good at it, too. Minnie Lou said her mother "was a great hand to draw pictures," and she enjoyed drawing, too. Minnie Lou drew pictures for the other schoolchildren. Mattie drew pictures of houses with pencil, also pen, and ink to give to the Sunshine People. They were a little like the Red Cross and maybe Christmas Cheer people, Minnie said. They

gave things to people who really needed them. Mattie's brothers mad[e] picture frames for the pictures.

John said the Sunshine People advertised in a local paper—po[or] people in need, didn't have a father to help with children, help was available from them. Mattie wrote to them, and the "first batch of things weren't fit for a dog." Mattie said they were probably testing them to see if they really needed help. She wrote back and thanked them for the clothes. The next batch, them was nice, good clothes.

Health, Cleanliness, Wellness At bath time (at least once a week), a sheet was hung up for privacy, and each one would take a bath next to the fireplace. Toothbrushes were made from dogwood and black gum trees. Most of the time, the children would brush their teeth on the way to school. They would break off a short twig, chew on one end, an[d] then brush with the frayed end. "Later, we had real tooth brushes," said Ida Ruth.

Minnie Lou said, "Mama loved flowers, and she had floral bouquets in the house year 'round. Lilacs in spring; daisies and zinnias in summer; chrysanthemums in fall, and in winter, tall grass that opene[d] to a fluffy bloom."

Other Helpers Anne Cary Bradley sent the Hollandsworth family clothes and other things they needed when they lived near Fayerdale. Ida Ruth had a picture of this elegant-looking lady.

About a mile or two from the farmhouse was Lester Robertson'[s] store. Each month Mr. Robertson gave them a 100 lb. sack of meal. He came by and set it off. One of the children would come out so he woul[d] know they saw it and got it.

Faith Healer   Mattie was a Faith Healer. She could "take out fire" and "stop blood." When a child or anyone was accidentally burned, they came to Mattie to take the fire out. The same with a bad cut, she stopped the bleeding. Mattie said she could share this secret with three people, no more. If told to a fourth person, she could no longer perform this amazing feat. One of her brothers could take off warts.

Somber Note   From Uncle Albert: "Bob Gusler made pretty coffins. No one was embalmed in those days.

Anne Cary Bradley

Ghosts, Witches, and Other Strange Things

One dark night the family heard an organ playing. Now, their organ was downstairs in the main room and no one was playing it. This music came from upstairs. They tiptoed up the stairs and upon reaching the top step, the music stopped. Shortly after that, Ed was drafted for the war. He was a private in the Army of World War I. He was stationed at Camp Lee and served nine months.

Another night when both Ed and Albert were away, there was a noise like someone walking up the plank walk, and it knocked at the door. So, Mattie pretended her brothers were there and called one of them to come downstairs. Whatever it was went away.

Mattie told the story about the gang of ducks in the yard at her old home-place. An old witch wanted the ducks. They wouldn't give them to her. The witch said, "Well, they won't ever do you any good!" Then, those ducks started dropping dead. Somebody accidentally stepped on one's foot when it fell and it was the only duck that didn't die. They never could keep but one duck after that.

Another witch story: you could draw a picture of a witch, shoot it, and it would cripple her. And here she would come hobbling along to borrow something. If you loaned her something, she would get all right.

Not all witches were female—some were male. One in Patrick County long ago was a colored man, and his wife was also a witch. Once a group of young folks were in the yard of Betsy Ingram's home talking about witches; one girl said she didn't believe in them. So, this male witch put a spell on her. To take it off, he gave her something to take to the river, turn around, throw it in the river, and not look back. The spe

went off, and went on a dog. It died.

There were witch doctors, too. They could cure a spell cast on

you by a witch. That is, if the witch was still living. If the witch that ca

the spell was dead, he couldn't take it off.

A witch doctor could tell what anyone had on before they got

there. One man asked him what his wife had on. He told the man it

was a cotton check dress. When they got to the house, she had on a

calico dress. The witch doctor declared, "That's the first time I ever go

fooled." The woman had seen them coming up the road and changed

dresses. She did have on a check dress.

Mattie and the sunken grave: Mattie and two of her sisters

were milking the cows at the family farm one evening—later than

usual—it was getting dark outside. Nannie finished before the others,

and said she was going to the house. When Mattie and Ruth finished

milking, they decided to take a shortcut through an old graveyard, and

get to the house before Nannie did. They climbed over the fence near

sunken grave. There was someone in the grave all doubled up, face

down. The girls figured it was Nannie trying to scare them, so they

tiptoed around the grave and hurried to the house. To their surprise,

Nannie was in the kitchen; she had already strained the milk, and was

waiting for them. Mattie and Ruth looked at each other, and silently

agreed not to tell Nannie about the grave they saw, because it might

frighten her into thinking she would die soon. Their looks also asked a

question: "If not Nannie, who was in that sunken grave?"

Another true story: Sam Martin's (Mattie's brother) horse got down sick, about dead. An old woman (witch) that lived in the hollow, borrowed something from Sam. He said that woman put a spell on his horse. So, Sam got a male witchdoctor (the good one I guess) to take the spell off. He told Sam, "She's gonna (sic) come back here and want to borrow something. Don't let her have anything, not even a grain of corn."

Shortly, here she comes. "Where's Sam Martin? I want to borrow something." Sam was hiding.

The male witch doctor said, "What is it, maybe I can help you."

"No, I got to see Sam Martin, want to borrow it from him"

Sam jumped out and said, "Here's old Samuel Isaac. You might as well get on back up the hill. You're not gonna (sic) borrow anything from me, not even a grain of corn." She begged, but he would not loan her anything. She went on back up the hill. They followed after her. There was a pine tree in her yard; a squirrel ran up and down it three times. They followed her into the house, and the old woman was dead.

Ed Turner

Illness, Herbs, Remedies

Heard here and there in interviews:

Jennie had scarlet fever. So did Jim. It made him temporarily deaf. One day he was missing, could not find him. Finally, here he comes, been rabbit hunting with the cat.

Ida Ruth had the flu in the 1918 worldwide flu epidemic (pandemic).* She had lockjaw, eyes rolled back, they thought she was dead. Jim prayed to God to "raise the dead." He pried her jaws open with a spoon and kept a vigil over her until she said, "I want some water."

Mullen, washed...put together with heart leaves, washed...boil, strong as coffee...down to one quart, add chunks of pine knots with resin...for TB.

Blood root (real poisonous) smells like iodine...good for blood poisoning. Cream (milk) and powdered copas (a medicine) for poison oak.

Rat's vein (grows wild in woods)...rheumatism...put whiskey...bear's foot (plant) in jar. Both good for making tea whiskey. Yellow root...stomach trouble...dried it and chewed roots.

Ginseng also for stomach. Star root...sold it...Minnie Lou did not know what it was for.

One time John had the flu real bad—was "plumb out of my head." He stood up and dived out of the bed—thought he was down at the old swimming hole, diving in the water. "Boy, that hurt," he said. "I'll never forget that."

They missed Green one day, found him asleep in the pasture under a bush. Looking for Ida Ruth one day, they found her asleep on the end of the porch.

It sounds like they really worked hard, and needed more sleep

*An old newspaper dated November 24, 1976 with Richmond (AP) dateline: "They called it Spanish influenza then, and it struck Virginia i mid-September, 1918. A few soldiers at Ft. Lee, near Petersburg, bega to cough and to run high fevers. Within a month, the state was under siege by the disease." They said the Virginia State Fair was canceled ai one in four funerals that winter was a flu victim.

Green Hollandsworth reading.

Moving to Bassett

In 1922, they did not make enough grain to feed the mules. Jim called it a "famine." John I. Woods the overseer –he looked after about 200 acres—that last year he wouldn't take anything for rent. He said, "You didn't make enough to eat." The land was poor—just "worked-out." They moved to Bassett in February 1923. The boys were old enough to work in the furniture factory. That was their plan. It was time to move. The old wagon was packed full with their belongings. They hitched up the two mules; John drove the wagon to Bassett. The rest of the family walked along side the wagon on the 18-mile trip. They were all happy to move from the country to the bustling town of Bassett.

And that is Grandma's story in the land where fairies cried tears of stone.

The Dollhouses.

Mattie and Avis Turner

Epilogue

The boys went to work in the furniture factory. The girls helped their mother with her new venture—a boarding house. Grandma Hollandsworth rented two houses from the Bassett's—one to live in and one for boarders. She cooked their meals and served them in the kitchen of her house. They did this for about 12 years. Her brother, Tom Turner, helped the family by giving potatoes, flour, and other foods from his store nearby.

The children grew up, married, and moved on to start their own families. My mother met my father, Clifford Carter, at Riverview Church in Bassett. They rode the train to Martinsville and were married on November 9, 1933 by Reverend Nelson M. Fox, Sr.

When the last child had married—Mattie Lee and Kern Coleman were moving to West Virginia—Grandma came to live with us on Third Street in North Bassett, about 1940. I was five, she was 60.

Through the years Grandma's ability to "make-do and be resourceful" carried into: a round table from bent willow branches; wood doll-size furniture, including: bed, chair, settee, rocking chair, round table with masonite top and legs from a forked tree branch; and animals from pine cones and pipe cleaners (turkey, ostrich). She made dollhouses from cardboard boxes with unbelievable details: mantle over fireplace, window sills, and porch light fixtures from old beads. She made three houses. My sister Edith and double-first cousin Peggy (Jim's daughter) got single-story Cape Cod houses and I got the two-story house (I suppose because I'm older). They all had dormer windows on the roof, chimneys, and were open in the back to put in little plastic furniture—from a real "dime store."

Grandma had a large goiter in her neck. She wore dresses with large necklines and pretty collars. Today, surgery will remove a goiter the early stages.

Our Grandma, Mattie Hollandsworth, died on June 2, 1958, age 78. Besides the golden earrings, that she never removed, I don't remember but one other piece of jewelry that Grandma had. It was a necklace made from a polished fairystone with gold tips.

Mattie about 1950

Excerpts from Interviews—1960s -1970s

James Robert Hollandsworth, son

"I was about twelve years old when my father died. I being the oldest of six children this meant that I should go foremost in helping my mother to make a living. At the age of twelve I could not get a public job."

"I learned to trap minks, muskrats, and skunks, and we would search the hills for ginseng, which sold for about $13.00 per pound."

"When I became sixteen years old, I began to work at the sawmill, and load tanbark*, and most anything I could do."

John Peter Hollandsworth, son

"We would set steel traps along the creek bank—trapped mink, we got $20 for one of these. Muskrat, skunk, possum, coon, fox— trapped them, skinned them and hung up to dry—then boxed them up and shipped to a company that bought the skins."

"Rabbit gums—we'd make double traps with partition in the middle, door on each end. Baited with salt, onions, apple peeling— sometimes have a possum in one end and a rabbit on the other end; sometimes two in the same end of trap. One especially cold morning— frost everywhere—had 16 rabbits in that trap!"

"...load tanbark* by moonlight until 11:00 or 12:00 at night— pay us $2.00/$2.50 per day.

"There was a ginseng patch ½ mile to the right of the old iron ore mine."

"We worked in stave (barrel) mill at Fayerdale, Jim and me. Bale staves—24 to a bale, and tie with wire."

"Two mules and a wagon—hauled cross ties to be sent to Bassett for the railroad. White oak—squared them up with hew ax—went on the train from Fayerdale to Philpott—then switched from Philpott to Bassett."

*Webster's dictionary states "tanbark is any bark containing tannin, used to tan hides..."

Minnie Lou Hollandsworth Foley, daughter

"My dad had a favorite dog, and when dad died, this dog went around the house to the place where dad slept and moaned and howle so pitiful, it seemed he said, 'Oh, Lord', so plain."

"We raised our own brooms. I remember when Mama plante the broomcorn, I once cut my finger on one of the stalks. I still carry th scar."

"We took rocks on boards and made play houses and covered them with moss and had moss rugs on the floor. They were very prett I remember Minnie Cox and Katherine Cox and many others would get me to make play houses for them at school."

"The time came the boys were old enough to work in a factory and we moved to Bassett. That was one of my happiest moments."

Thomas Green Hollandsworth, son

"In answer to your letter, thank you for being interested as you have heard about how I learned to count."

"The first day of school for me I took a first reader also a third reader, but I came to class with the third grade book and they laughed, but not for long, for I could read as well as the rest."

"We farmed with a team of mules. If I could have some of the things to eat now as the old times, I would enjoy it. But we had to work long and hard on the farm as in the years of World War I. We had no electricity; had to cut wood for fuel."

"I went to the mountains by myself at 10 years of age, hunted ginseng. Sometimes I would get about six dollars worth."

Mattie Lee Hollandsworth Coleman, daughter

"I remember we had a rocking chair without arms."

"We used to carry a small dog named Waddley to school and we dressed him in clothes for a baby. Katherine and Minnie Cox used to play with us. We took turns riding their ponies."

"Mama gathered us around her and she would read the Bible."

"Minnie had a song book and she would ask me to sing with her. At times I didn't want to, and Minnie slapped my face and said, 'sing now', but I think it turned into another tune."

Ida May (called Ida Ruth), Hollandsworth Carter Foley, daughter

"I am the seventh child of Martha Ellen Turner and Thomas Alexander Hollandsworth, born in Franklin County on January 20, 1913 at home in a new log cabin my dad built—it is covered now by Philpot Lake."

"We made mud furniture while the cow ate grass. One day a snake crawled down between us and Lee (Mattie Lee) jumped up and said, 'Lordy, I am bit'. The snake just crawled on—we were okay."

"We climbed chinquapin trees to shake them out, also picked up chestnuts, and little sweet balls on oak trees—we knew the good ones to pick."

"Most people had a mattress filled with corn shucks or straw in the olden days."

Author's note: My mother's name is Ida May in the family Bible, but Grandma's sister, Ruth Anna Elizabeth Turner Stone said, "If you don't name her Ida Ruth after me, I will have nothing to do with her." I did not know for a very long time that my mother's true name was Ida May and not Ida Ruth as everyone called her.

Excerpts of visit, November 2, 1973
Albert Lee Turner, brother

Mattie was 16 years old when her brother Albert was born. In 1915, Albert was 19 years old and Mattie told him he could board with her for 50 cents a day. He said, "But Matt, that's all I make at the saw mill." Of course, she knew that and was teasing him. "All my sister

wanted was help in the fields and a man in the house for protection."
His brother Ed had died the year before (this visit) on May 6, 1972, age
78. He is buried in Old Center church cemetery.

Author's note: I had two children under ten years old, but that should
not be an excuse to not interview everyone you can, when the story is
one you really care about. How I wish I had visited my great-uncle
Edward Daniel Turner.

I interviewed two of Grandma's brothers when I was taking an
independent study course in genealogy from Brigham Young University,
Utah, in 1979.

Joshua Thomas Turner, age 94—born April 17, 1885

I asked Uncle Tom how he met his wife, Ida Stone. He said she
lived near his sister Matt and husband Tom Hollandsworth. Ida's
mother was Tom's sister, Nancy Elizabeth "Betty" Frances
Hollandsworth who married James Abraham Stone. Uncle Tom said he
boarded with Matt and Tom—20 cents a day in 1908—besides being
near Ida, he also worked with Tom Hollandsworth cutting stave wood
and cross ties.

He watched Ida grow up (she was born August 11, 1893, eight
years younger than Uncle Tom). When she turned 19, they were
married—on November 20, 1912 and had a family of nine children
(including a set of twins). Ida died January 1, 1974, age 81. Uncle Tom
died January 25, 1990, almost 105 years old.

George James Turner, age 96—born October 10, 1883

He liked to pitch horseshoes when a young lad; could beat any of the rest. Uncle George met his wife, Hattie Ann Turner (daughter o Ira Tazewell Turner and Sarah Jane Bryant) at a dance (young people took turns hosting dances in their homes). They were married April 3, 1904, and had a family of ten children.

Uncle George was also a Faith Healer. Like his sister, Matt, he could take out fire and stop blood, but he could take off warts too. He worked as a miller on the mountain. Later, he built a house at Bassett Forks, and a mill nearby to grind corn for meal. Once he had 30 acres corn, now only 10. He used to sell corn meal for 5 cents a pound. Wh grinding corn for others, say, eight bushels—he would get one bushel as his fee.

They had a big bell outside the back door. Hattie used to ring i when George and the boys were in the field to tell them dinner (the noon meal) was ready. It also was rung when a customer came to the mill and he could go to grind the corn. Hattie was born June 27, 1886 and died March 27, 1968, age 82. Uncle George died January 23, 1982, age 98.

Notes from interviews and research:

Elmer Haynes states in his book, *The Fayerdale Tragedy Fairy Stone State Park* that Euel Cox never smoked or drank. "He always said you could not drink and run a business."

Euel Cox General Merchandise Store and his home were about three miles from Fayerdale. Cox was a very prosperous farmer, merchant, and bootlegger. He was ambushed in 1922 by three men. He shot one of the attackers, one shot him, and the third escaped and left the area. Euel Cox died September 6, 1922, little more than 24 hours after the shootings, age 35. There was a big trial. Dr. A. C. Lancaster was the first witness. Cox was a veteran of World War I, and was at Camp Lee in Virginia, as was Mattie's brother, Ed Turner.

Article by Horace G. Brown, Martinsville Bulletin reprinted the 1948 article July 4, 1976.

He went to Fayerdale in 1906 and worked for the Virginia Ore and Lumber Company as storekeeper and payroll clerk.

"The T. C. DeHart Distilling Company of Woolwine...used to haul by wagon hundreds of barrels of whiskey and brandy for us to sip and ship to various parts of the United States."

World Book Encyclopedia: Prohibition. The 18th amendment signed in 1917, took effect June 16, 1920..."forbidding by law of the sale, and sometimes manufacture of alcoholic beverages..." The amendment was repealed in February 1933. This was Amendment 21 (to the Constitution of the United States).

Fairy Stone State Park Brochure "The Iron Mine Trail...there was whisk making, both legal and illegal. One could make whiskey legally by purchasing a government stamp for about $1.50 per gallon.

Poems by "Bradley" (Honorable Daniel Hillsman Wood) & The Fayerda Story compiled by Ora Mae Pilson Hylton. Daniel H. Wood lived about three miles from the Fairy Stone Park area. Several of his poems are about the boomtown of Fayerdale. "A stave (barrel stave) mill was operated by Edward Jefferson Philpott." "P. T. Setliff, now a merchant Collinsville, was mine foreman."

P. T. (Peter Thomas) Setliff married Ada Lou Bryant. He was born about 1887, and died in March of 1963. P. T. Setliff and his wife lived near us in Collinsville in the 1940s and 1950s. I did not know until Ora's book in 1988 that he worked in Fayerdale. We used to walk to his little store (located on a lower portion of where the Collinsville Shopping Center parking lot is today) crossing Rt. 220 (probably a two-lane road then). Nothing was more refreshing than a cold Grapette® from the chest-type drink machine—reaching down in the icy water the soft drinks were in and using the opener on the front to get the bottle cap off. Mr. and Mrs. Setliff lived in the back of the store. We enjoyed the convenience of the store, also just visiting with our neighbors.

One of my favorite television shows was The Walton's in the 1970s. I have some on video tapes. I saved many of the show's descriptions in TV Guide, and have been on a bus trip to visit Walton's Mountain Museum, home of "John Boy" in Schuyler, Virginia in Nelson County (near Charlottesville). Real-life John-Boy Earl Hamner turned his experiences as a boy into this successful television program.

During one particular show, I made a few notes. It went something like this: Mary Ellen was doing volunteer work for the Sunshine People—kind of like the Red Cross, and they deliver boxes to folks at Christmas, she said. Mary Ellen noticed a drawing on her teacher's desk one day—of their school building. Mary Ellen asks, "Did a student draw this? It's very good. It must be nice to have lots of time to just draw pretty pictures." The teacher tells Mary Ellen that her friend who works with the Sunshine People gave it to her and said, "T lady who drew this picture is a widow with six children."

Ida Ruth always had pretty flowers at every house she lived in My sister, Edith, and I especially enjoyed the hollyhocks. She showed how to make dolls from the flowers, turned upside down. They looke like elegant ladies in gowns, maybe even little dancing Fairies.

I saved this obituary. Audella "Della" Wood Harger died June 1987, age 105, daughter of Hillsman and Ruth Corn Wood. Widow of Walter Harger, former Patrick County teacher and former Patrick County School Board member, survived by several nieces and nephew

Today, at Fairy Stone you will find programs such as these liste among others for September 2010: Lake Explorers, Roost in Peace (about bats), Night Hike, Fairy Stone Hunt, Fairy Houses/Gnome Home (built by participants of all ages).

I read about this in the Martinsville Bulletin's Stroller column. The Bassett Historical Center always has interesting displays and exhibits. I especially enjoyed seeing the Diorama of Fayerdale Exhibit i the Spring of 2006. The miniature scenes of 1911 Fayerdale were mad by retired Navy Captain John P. "Jack" Williamson of Williamsburg, Virginia.

The exact layout is not known because there are no surviving photographs or written histories; only verbal histories by former residents, and a few newspaper articles, the Stroller said. Included in Williamson's depiction are Virginia Ore and Lumber Company offices, railroad lines, freight depot, water tower, a company store and post office; and the distilling warehouse. There was the "modern" bandsaw mill on Goblintown Creek where my grandfather Hollandsworth worked. I could imagine my mother and her siblings walking with hands behind their back, just looking at everything in the store, as their mama had instructed.

Jack Williamson's seven page of History of Fayerdale, Virginia ends with "Fayerdale vanished into the mountain mists." Instead, there is "a delightfully pure and rustic mountain retreat where one may hike the paths of miners and moonshiners, peer into an abandoned iron mine, and swim, boat and fish in a beautiful woodland lake where once there was a town and two railroads."

Mattie in later years.

Related Articles

From a Research Paper by Aleta Turner, a senior at Bassett High School, April 1986:

The Civilian Conservation Corps

When Franklin Delano Roosevelt accepted the presidential nomination in 1932, he told of his personal plans for national conservation. Roosevelt planned to fight soil erosion and declining timber resources by using young people who were, literally, wandering aimlessly in a jobless country. Some were recent high school graduates, and unable to meet the expenses of a college education. As a father of four young sons, Roosevelt had for a long time been interested in an educational system that would provide a combination of intellectual exercise, manual training, and financial independence.

Stimulated by his longtime interests in forestry and conservation, Roosevelt proposed to take 250,000 unemployed young men (girls were excluded from the program) off the streets and welfare rolls and give them jobs at $30 a month plus keep for doing useful work in forests and national parks. His inspiration came from the American philosopher, William James, who had written about the wisdom of training our young people for constructive instead of destructive work in an article entitled "The Moral Equivalent for War."

One of the programs authorized in the First Hundred Days was the Emergency Conservation Work Act. It was more commonly known as the Civilian Conservation Corps or just the CCC and was a favorite project of President Roosevelt. Organized quickly by the War Department, ten days after the CCC was proposed on March 21, 1933, it was the law, and by July, over 300,000 boys were off the roads and int Roosevelt's "peace camps" where they were to serve their country in civilian rather than military capacity. They began working on such projects as land clearance, forestry, land reclamation, building dams, planting trees, repairing roads, building and improving state and national parks, even fighting forest fires. Instead of guns and grenade Roosevelt's "Tree Army" used picks, axes, and shovels.

Facts and Figures:

The National Director was Robert Fechner who was appointed April 5, 1933. The first CCC camp opened near Luray, Virginia with an enrollment of 2500. The first enrollee, Henry Rich, was inducted April 1933. The CCC boys built stone cottages in Maryland, which became Camp David.

At its peak there were 500,000 young people employed by the CCC. Two and a half million men served in the CCC before Congress abolished it in 1942. Two million of those men are alive today (1981 newspaper article). Four thousand camps, in all states, and also Hawai Alaska (they became states later), Puerto Rico, and the Virgin Islands.

The CCC boys served as Honor Guard for the 1939 visit of the King and Queen of England. CCC boys were "co-stars" in a movie callec "The Army in Overalls."

3,470 fire towers were erected. 97,000 miles of truck roads were built. More than 40,000 illiterates were taught to read and write. More than two billion, three hundred million trees were planted.

Fairy Stone State Park in nearby Patrick County was built by the CCC in the 1930s. They built the log cabins for visitors, park maintenance buildings, and the lake itself. Many people in Virginia and surrounding states enjoy this park today—more than 50 years later.

Aleta Turner, 1986, Great granddaughter of Mattie Hollandsworth
Fairy Stone Interpretive Staff, September 9, 1986:

"Special thanks should also be extended to Aleta Turner for the use of her fascinating paper on Fayerdale. The paper was on display all summer and many people gained information from her research."

Martinsville Bulletin, February 23, 2011:

"Virginia will celebrate the 75th Anniversary of the state park system with special programs, contests, activities, souvenirs, and a birthday cake. Fairy Stone Park was one of the original six parks. There are now 35 parks with more than 8 million visitors from around the world."

Iron ore mine at Fairy Stone State Park.

Looking Backward column, by Avis Turner, Stuart Enterprise, April 10, 1974.

Over in neighboring Franklin County is a big rock—it is called Calico Rock. Much of it is now submerged under the waters of the Philpott Reservoir. But it used to be 500 feet from the top down to the creek below. I know, because my great grandfather measured it with a 500 ft. spool of his wife's sewing thread. His name was Robert Turner, but everyone called him Robin. He was born July 14, 1852. He married Sarah Ellen Martin May 20, 1872. Robin and Sarah had a little house about a mile from Calico Rock. Like most everyone else in those days farming was their way of life. To supplement this, Robin cut and sold the timber on his land. Large trees were felled with axes and crosscut saws. Then they were cut into logs 2 ½ feet long. This was the length of barrel staves—they were called stavewood blocks. He rolled these big logs over Calico Rock. They would swing out and come back, hit the rock, split up and land at the bottom of Calico Rock. Then he would drive the wagon down below and split the billets up to be delivered to a stavewood mill where they were made into staves for the purpose of making barrels to hold flour. I understand it was quite a "show" to watch those logs coming off the top of Calico Rock from down below— safely out of the way, of course.

Robin's oldest son, Willie, decided to climb down the steepest part of Calico Rock one day. About half way down he got his finger caught between the rocks and thought he was a gonner. Willie finally got his finger loose and continued his way down to the creek below.

Calico Rock was a favorite picnic and fishing spot when I was growing up—in the 1940s—before Philpott Dam was built. Every East Monday, we went up with aunts, uncles, cousins, and friends for an al day outing. We took long walks, had a picnic lunch, and fished in the waters below majestic Calico Rock.

Looking Backward column by Avis Turner, Stuart Enterprise, February 1975.

One source says Union Church was organized in 1815. The firs church record is dated Saturday, November 17, 1821 and states, "Ther met Brethren Jesse Jones, John Conner and Peter Howard as a presbytery and after divine service constituted the Church of Christ at Union Meeting house in Patrick County, Virginia, consisting of the following male members: Brethren John Washborne, John Foster, Richard Massey, William Walden, Jeremiah Burnett, Randolph Cox, Nicholas Grimmet, James Ingram, William Turner, Francis Cox, Alexander Ingram, 11 male members. Sisters Jane Turner, Selah Hand Martha Ingram, Elizabeth Ingram, Jane Cox, Elizabeth Burnett, Margar Walden, Susanna Foster, eight females, total 19 members."

Old Union is a church of the Primitive Baptist (sometimes calle Old-School Baptist) faith. Some of its ministers have been: Stephen Hubbard, the first pastor; John Washborne, ordained to the ministry in 1823, John Turner, 1824; Jeremiah Burnett, 1825; Joshua Adams, 1833

76

A. J. Cassell, 1865; Peter Corn, 1868; P. A. Cahill, 1884, and E. R. Bryant who was pastor for more than 25 years.

I can remember going to Union Church when I was growing up. It was a lovely and simple church of white clapboards and shaded by tall trees. Located above Fairy Stone Park, Union Church sat right beside Smith River. There was an old swinging bridge to the other side. Baptizings were held here in front of the church. Sometimes they had all-day meetings with dinner on the grounds. For use in the summer months there were weathered benches and a pulpit built outside. Services were held out-of-doors when hundreds of people attended communion and meetings of the church association. At these large meetings, concession stands were set up. Nearby storekeepers sold ice cream, candy, cold drinks, and watermelons.

My family used to go with friends to the Union Church area for all-day outings. We fished in the river near Union Bridge, collected pretty rocks, played ball in a nearby field and ate our picnic lunch on the wooden steps of Old Union Church.

The original church and bridge are now under water— submerged by the waters of Smith River that backed up over 4,000 acres in Franklin, Henry, and Patrick Counties when Philpott Dam was built twenty-some years ago. A new church was built and a new bridge, too. Elder Leonard Brammer of Fieldale is now pastor of Union Church.

Looking Backward column, by Avis Turner, Stuart Enterprise, February 19, 1975.

In the old days washday came around on the same day every week—usually Monday. It was a little different from now as we can wash any day we want—just take your hamper full of clothes to the basement or laundry room, add store-bought detergent and push a fe buttons. Then dry them equally as easy in an automatic dryer.

In Grandma's day, clothes were washed outside. In winter, some people washed inside in the kitchen where it was warm. Water was brought by bucket from the creek or spring or maybe they'd caug rainwater in a barrel. The water was heated in a big, black, iron pot; a blazing fire underneath. When the water was hot, it was dipped into the washing tub mixing cold water and hot water until it was just right Then you added the homemade soap and started scrubbing on the old washboard. Before the wooden and then corrugated metal washboar were invented, clothes were "battled." That is, beat on a large block o wood with wooden paddles. While scrubbing colored clothes on the washboard, white clothes were boiling in the iron pot. An old broom handle, bleached from countless immersions, was used to punch them up and down through the soapy water and to lift gingerly from the hot water.

Clothes were rinsed in two or three tubs of cold water. To mai white clothes whiter a mixture called "bluing" was added to the last rinse. Starch was made from a mixture of flour and water, then boiled until it reached the consistency needed—thick for doilies, then thinnec with water for dresses.

After all the clothes had been soaked, scrubbed, boiled, and rinsed, they were hung on fences, bushes, and grass to dry. The soapy water was then "recycled" by scrubbing the kitchen or porch floors. Rinse water was poured over the flowerbeds.

My grandmother used to make her own soap—with lye and grease. Here's another trick she used in later years to make a "new" bar of soap from all the scraps she'd saved in a tightly covered jar: Cut or grate into very small pieces. Barely cover them with boiling water to soften. In about 20 minutes, or when cool enough, mash with a fork and work with hands to shape into a bar of soap. When dry, wrap loosely in wax paper until needed.

Looking Backward column, by Avis Turner, Stuart Enterprise, March 5, 1975.

Sarah Ellen Martin was born December 4, 1855. She was the 19th child born to Elder William M. Martin and Nancy Adams Martin. When Sarah Ellen was 16, she married (on May 20, 1872) 19 year-old Robert Turner, the son of Josiah Turner, Jr. and Malinda Ingram Turner. Robert had no middle name, but was called "Robin." Robin and Sarah had 14 children, including my grandmother, Martha Ellen called "Mat." Sarah gave her sons two names as she did my grandmother, but her other three daughters received three names each: Nancy Susan Evaline, Ruth Anna Elizabeth, and Dollie Malinda Mary.

My great grandmother was a midwife. She delivered many babies in the Dodson community of Patrick County. Part of a letter she wrote to my grandmother is revealing of this job: "Mattie I will write you a few lines to let you hear from me I got home all right but I did n

get to rest before I had to go to Dick Glaspyes I had good luck and

Floence has a fine boy. Mattie I was so tired when I got home I did no

go to preaching..."

In her letters, there were no periods and very few capitals.

Words were spelled like they sound.

Sarah Ellen wrote poetic obituaries. Some were published in

The Messenger of Truth (a religious magazine of the Primitive Baptists

She was a member of Union Church, joining in 1887. I have seen her

name spelled Sarah and Sharah. On some letters, she signed them

Sharah or just S. E. Turner.

She used to go fishing before breakfast to catch suckers with a

string and hook. She would lie down on a rock beside the creek and

ease out the line, catch a fish and ease it in. A bent straight pin was he

hook. Soon she was on her way back home to cook the fish for

breakfast.

One day in the early part of 1907, Sarah Ellen Martin Turner go

on her horse and rode off to Ferrum. She went to get some paint for

the house. On the way home, she was caught in a terrible rainstorm

and caught the "galloping consumption." She was confined to her bed

for three months and died May 23, 1907 at the age of 51.

Recipe sent to Good Old Days magazine, published in Winter 1976 issue.

FRIED APPLE PIES

Yummy pies from my grandmother's kitchen.

1 quart bag dried apples

2 cups water

½ cup sugar

½ teaspoon cinnamon

Wash apples, add water, and cook in saucepan 25 minutes. Mash with potato masher. Add sugar and cinnamon. Use pie dough or biscuit dough for crust. Roll out real thin. Cut out circles the size of a saucer. Put one to two tablespoons apples on one-half of pie circle. Moisten edges with water, fold over, pinch edges together and prick with fork. Fry in shortening on both sides until light brown or until dough is cooked. Makes 10 large pies.

Mrs. Avis C. Turner, Rt. 5, Box 129, Bassett, Virginia 24055

Bent Willow Table with Smoky, the cat, on top. Below, The Calico Roc

Author's Notes on Chestnut Trees

Sometime in the early 1900s, a blight began to destroy the mighty chestnut tree. For the Hollandsworth family, chestnuts were a staple on their rented farm—for food and a product to sell or trade; and the men worked in the forest and at sawmills to produce railroad ties.

In a Mother Earth News, Aug/Sept, 1998 article by Dr. Charles Dikson tells us the chestnut tree was called the "redwood of the east." It was plentiful and was used for telephone poles, railroad ties, and furniture. A fungus caused the blight that spread 50 miles each year and killed all trees in its path. By the 1940s, all eastern forests were affected and the chestnut was all but extinct.

The American Chestnut Foundation was established in the 1950s to support research and to study the root system, which was not affected by the blight.

A July 14, 2011 Martinsville Bulletin article by Ashley Jackson tells of a local experiment with a blight-resistant American chestnut—a two foot tall sapling was planted at Philpott Lake in 2009 is now about five feet tall.

Since the blight did not kill the root, many saplings grow, but at about 15 to 20 feet high, the blight kills the tree. We hope the scientists' "backcross method of plant breeding transferring the blight-resistance of the Chinese chestnut to the American chestnut" is successful.

DATE 1967

PLACE Fairystone park

OCCASION

This is where our mailbox was when we lived here.

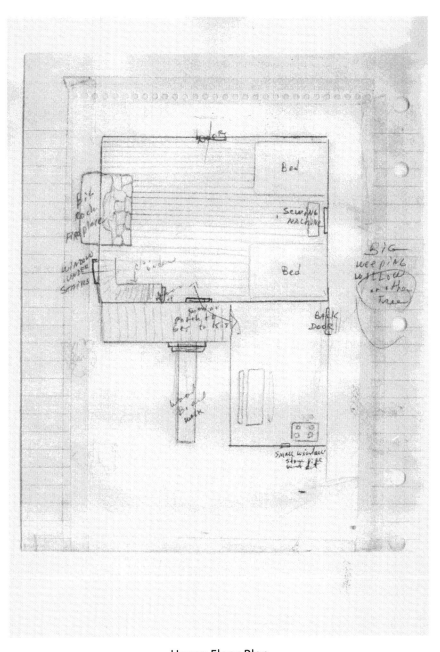

House Floor Plan

I remember

Washing at the spring
with wash board and tub.
— Hanging clothes on
bushes —

Water ran through
box & kept milk cool

ROCK PLAY
HOUSE

MUD
FURNITURE

spring milk box

Mattie's drawings

The snake and the girls

The Rock Chimney and girls giggling

Mattie's chair and table

Sitting in a sandbox, on Third Street in the northern part of Bassett where the factory now rests along the Smith River, is Avis Eller Carter now Turner, the daughter of Clifford and Ida Hollandsworth Carter and wife of Elbert Turner.

About Avis Turner

Avis Turner was born in her grandmother's house in Bassett, Virginia. Her family was among the first residents of Collinsville in the 1940s. She graduated from Fieldale High School in 1952, and received a two year Secretarial Certificate from Radford College in 1954. She has taken classes in creative writing at Patrick Henry Community College and independent study courses on writing and genealogy. Avis Turner has worked as a secretary, library aide, and bookmobile librarian. She published The Carter Family Tree in 1984. Her articles have been published in magazines and books including Grit, Women's Household, Virginia Microfilm News, Patrick County Heritage Books, and the Henry County Virginia Heritage Book. The next project is writing about her mother's diary, the boarding house, and life in Bassett in the 1930s.

Photo by Jeanette Daniel

91

The Villanelle

This poetic form was mentioned at a meeting of the Piedmo

Writers Group. From Wikipedia: "A villanelle has only two rhy

sounds. The first and third lines of the first stanza are rhyming refra

that alternate as the third line in each successive stanza and form

couplet at the close...nineteen lines long."

I'd been working on "Grandma's Story" —she was born in 18

and lived in the Fayerdale area (now Fairy Stone State Park) when I r

across notes on the Villanelle. It "entered English language poetry in t

1800s from the imitation of French models." Intrigued, I began t

poem as a memorial to my grandmother, Martha Ellen Turr

Hollandsworth.

All that's left
is a slab of marble.
I remember more.

Grandmother/"single" mom/widow.
Photographs, mementoes,
All that's left.

Seamstress, farmhand, cook,
Faith Healer, sister, daughter,
I remember more.

Church member, neighbor.
Hard worker, dawn to dusk.
All that's left:

Dollhouse from a box,
Turkey from a pine cone.
I remember more.
Memoirs, scrapbooks.
A marble monument.
All that's left.
I remember more.

Published *In Frame Visual Arts Magazine*

Issue 6, Jan. 2012

www.inframevisualarts.com

Acknowledgements

Big Thank You to my sister, Edith Hinton, and double-first cousin, Peggy Pegram, for their help in proofreading this little family tree book. They both helped in rewriting some of the paragraphs so they made more sense to the reader. We three had great fun on a 201 trip to the Fairy Stone State Park area on the Iron Mine Trail, remembering our grandmother and the hard life she must have had. Sometimes I feel overwhelmed in our modern world. I think of my grandmother, and say, "She survived, so can I."

The Bassett Historical Center has always been there when I need help for all the different family lines I am working on. I especially enjoyed the Diorama displayed in 2006. Made by Jack Williamson, it represents Fayerdale about six years after the town was established a an iron mining and lumbering center. Included were the railroad, freig depot, Euel Cox General Merchandise Store, and the sawmill where m grandfather worked.

I thank this book's publisher, Tom Perry, for his encouragemer and friendship.

Avis Turner

44739060R00056

Made in the USA
Charleston, SC
06 August 2015